144 Ways

to

WALK THE TALK

Eric Harvey and Al Lucia

WALK THE TALK.COM

Resources for Personal and Professional Success

Introduction

Acting in accord with our beliefs and values – **walking the talk** – is one of the greatest challenges each of us faces every day. It's true for individuals in all aspects of life … and equally true for organizations of every kind and size.

Most organizations *talk* good management through their stated mission, vision, and values. These displays of good intentions are excellent reminders of what we stand for. But the real worth of our values comes from what is practiced rather than what is merely professed. It's how we actually *behave* that ultimately defines our success and determines how we will be judged.

144 Ways to Walk The Talk is a collection of practical strategies to add to your repertoire of values-driven leadership practices. Each page begins with one of thirty-six behaviors common to highly effective individuals who walk their talk … and get the results they want. For each behavior, you'll find four action items and/or ideas to help you personally bring that behavior to life.

We recommend you read *144 Ways* with a highlighter in hand. Mark the strategies that seem applicable to you. Then select three you will begin working on. Each time you implement one of your selected strategies, add another to your list. That way, you'll have three ideas working at all times.

Use the blank lined pages provided in the back to record other **walk the talk** behaviors that you practice or observe in others. These additions will help make this handbook your personal reference guide to values-driven leadership.

Finally, as you begin to apply the ideas and techniques presented in this invaluable handbook, remember this:

> ## walking the talk is a journey – not a destination.

The fact that you never fully arrive is not important. What *is* important is that you continue moving in the right direction.

We wish you good fortune on your continuing journey of walking the talk. And we thank you for taking us along.

Eric Harvey and Al Lucia

As you read this book, you'll come across our **Solution Finder!**

Visit **WalkTheTalk.com** where you can immediately access our free tips to help you achieve personal and professional success!

WALKTHETALK.COM

Resources for Personal and Professional Success

Helping individuals and organizations, worldwide, achieve success through Values-Based Practices

To order additional copies of this handbook,
or for information on other
WALK THE TALK® products and services,
contact us at **1.888.822.9255**
or visit our website at **www.walkthetalk.com**

144 Ways to Walk The Talk (SECOND EDITION)

The WALK THE TALK Company
1100 Parker Square, Suite 250
Flower Mound, Texas 75028
972.899.8300

WALK THE TALK books are available at quantity discounts with bulk purchases for educational, business, or sales promotion use.

WALK THE TALK® and The WALK THE TALK® Company are registered trademarks of Performance Systems Corporation.

ISBN-13: 978-1-885228-91-8
ISBN-10: 1-885228-91-0

Printed in the United States of America
10 9 8 7 6 5 4 3 2 1

Printed by MultiAd

Contents ... THE BEHAVIORS

Words to live by
(and lead by)
are just words …
unless you actually
LIVE by them.
You have to
WALK THE TALK!

Develop and Maintain Technical Knowledge

Knowledge is the only instrument of production
that is not subject to diminishing returns.
~ J. M. Clark

1 Dedicate a minimum of two hours per week to enhancing your technical knowledge. Consider activities such as reading, observing, listening, and doing. The key here is *dedicated* time and focus.

2 **Divide and conquer.** Work as a team to stay abreast of technology advancements. For example: a) Divide the reading of trade and professional journals among your work group and request they highlight key information prior to passing the publication on to others; b) Ask others to share key learning from all workshops and conferences they attend – and training programs and webinars they participate in.

3 Volunteer for projects that will likely increase your knowledge, skills, marketability, and value to the organization.

4 Actively participate in professional associations. Most groups offer e-newsletters, journals, monthly meetings, blogs, and opportunities to network with others in your profession. These groups provide great opportunities to keep up with new developments – usually for a reasonable membership fee.

Adopt an Orientation to Action and Results

Apply yourself. Get all the education you can, but then, by God, do something. Don't just stand there, make it happen.
~ Lee Iacocca

5   Focus on results-oriented processes and outcomes that add value to the organization, rather than on "staying busy" activities and events that merely consume time.

6   Create a list of desired results ("end states") when planning tasks and projects. By evaluating potential activities against this list, you'll maintain focus and increase your chances of achieving the results you want.

7   Go on a **Work Safari** once a week. Hunt for an important task that needs to be done ... and do it. Then place it in an imaginary trophy case. You'll soon develop a reputation as a great "hunter."

8   Tackle important, high-priority tasks first – even though they may be the ones you least like to do. Save the fun work as a reward for handling the tougher issues.

Expect
Top Performance

High expectations are the key to everything!
~ Sam Walton

9   Be conscious of the **Self-Fulfilling Prophecy.** When you expect something to happen (positive or negative), you unconsciously act in a manner which makes that thing more likely to occur.

10   Involve your team in setting standards that are achievable but also require everyone to stretch their knowledge and skills. Avoid settling for mediocre or sub-par work. Remember that regardless of what you say, it is the performance you're willing to accept that becomes your true standard.

11   Think of each member of your work group as a high jumper. Celebrate the reaching of new heights – then "raise the bar," together. But don't forget, as you're raising that bar, so is your competition.

12   Make sure you *WALK* **THE TALK**. Earn the right to hold others to high standards by meeting them yourself.

FREE ... 10 Reasons Why Leaders Should Model the Commitment and Positive Attitudes They Expect From Others

Go to *www.walkthetalk.com*
(Click on "Free Resources")

Commit to Quality and Continuous Improvement

There's always room for improvement –
it's the biggest room in the house.

~ Louise Heath Leber

13 Adopt **The 10% Rule.** Set a personal goal to improve everything you're involved in by merely ten percent. Small improvements ARE "doable" and add up quickly.

14 Focus on *people* as well as processes. Keep in mind that quality is ultimately a matter of individual performance. It happens one day at a time … one person at a time.

15 Recognize and reward those who make improvements to products, processes, and services. Remember …

What gets celebrated, gets repeated!

16 **Sponsor a Quality Art Show.** Ask each team member to contribute a visual representation of what quality and continuous improvement means/looks like to him or her. Then display the "works of art" in a common area or on your organization's intranet. This creative exercise is a fun way to involve everyone in spreading and reinforcing the quality message.

Be Customer Driven

It is not the employer who pays the wages. Employers only handle the money. It is the customer who pays the wages.
~ Henry Ford

17 Adopt the following mindsets: a) Everyone you interact with at work is either an internal or external customer; and b) If your customers ever stop needing you, so will your organization.

18 Learn from "horror stories." Ask team members to share personal examples of receiving poor service – along with the impact it had on both them (the customer) and the service provider. Discuss what could have turned them into success stories.

19 Deliver what the customer actually wants rather than what you think they ought to have. If you're not sure what they want, ask!

20 Build **Business Partnerships** with your customers by under-promising, over-delivering, and following-up to ensure they are satisfied. Solicit their input on how your products and services can be improved.

 Solution FINDER

FREE ... A Letter to Every Employee About the Importance of Customer Service

Go to *www.walkthetalk.com*
(Click on "Free Resources")

Commit to Self-Development

*I don't think much of a man who is not
wiser today than he was yesterday.*
~ Abraham Lincoln

21 Become a **Continuous Learning Machine.** Set a personal
goal to learn something new about your job, about your
organization, or about your professional discipline every week.

22 Encourage others to pursue self-development activities.
Make time and resources available for them to enhance
their knowledge and job skills.

23 **Learn by Teaching.** Volunteer to be an instructor for
organizational training programs. You'll not only develop
in-depth knowledge about subjects you prepare to teach,
you'll also be able to help others develop and grow.

24 Look beyond your profession. Consider pursuing developmental activities that have nothing to do with your job, but
can help you grow as a person. You'll probably be surprised
at how much "unrelated" learning can positively impact your
job performance.

Make Timely and Values-Driven Decisions

The purpose of our value statements is to guide
both our behaviors and our decisions.
WALK THE TALK ... And Get The Results You Want

25 Do your best to avoid the decision-making extremes: Knee-Jerk Reactions (acting too quickly without considering alternatives or all the facts) and Paralysis of Analysis (stalling a decision with too much analysis and research). Remember that no decision is a "no" decision.

26 Involve those who must implement decisions in the decision-making process. Consider the ideas and opinions of those who *do* the work – they frequently know best and have a great deal to contribute. In addition, they'll be much more likely to support decisions they help make.

27 Become an "In-Sync-Erator." Ensure your decisions are in sync with organizational values *before* you implement them. If there's a conflict, pursue alternatives that are a better match with stated values.

28 When announcing a decision, always explain the *reason* for it ... and the *process* used to arrive at it.

Staying in Shape

Looking to build or strengthen your leadership "muscles"?
Here are some exercises ... **TO AVOID:**

Jumping to conclusions

Passing the buck

Grabbing the credit

Throwing your weight around

Stretching the truth

Bending the rules

Breaking your promises

Playing favorites

Stepping on others

Dodging your duty

Running your mouth off

Plugging your ears

Side-stepping problems

Shooting down the organization

Pulling others into your funk

Holding others back

Pressing "my way or else"

Just *skating* by

Solve Problems
Effectively

Additional problems are the offspring of poor solutions.
~ Mark Twain

29 Adopt **The Solution-Plus-One Rule.** Develop and consider at least *two* solutions for every issue or problem you face. Don't "run" with the first idea that comes into your mind – unless you're sure that it's the very best play.

30 Conduct a "pro-versus-con" analysis on all proposed solutions. Consider all relevant facts and issues – as well as the probable perceptions of the people who will be impacted. Eliminate those solutions with significantly more downsides.

31 Avoid negative returns by making sure the ultimate cost of the solution (money, time, effect on others, etc.) is *less* than the cost of the problem.

32 Seek "win-win" solutions. Whenever possible, adopt those solutions through which the most people are positively impacted … and the fewest are negatively affected.

Be Flexible

An oak and a reed were arguing about their strength.
When a strong wind came up, the reed avoided being
uprooted by bending and leaning with the gusts of wind.
But the oak stood firm and was torn up by the roots.
~ Aesop

33 Encourage others to break tradition, when appropriate, in order to find better ways of doing things. Remember: If you continue doing what you've always done, you'll continue to get the same results.

34 Understand and appreciate that others may not do things exactly as you would do them. Be open-minded ... you might discover *their* way is even better.

35 Eliminate "Stop Signs to Progress" by avoiding statements such as:

We've tried that before!
That's not the way we do that here!
That will never work!

36 Don't cast all decisions in cement. Be willing to modify them as changing circumstances or data dictate.

Support
Risk Taking

Behold the turtle. He makes progress only when he sticks his neck out.
~ James B. Conant

37 Work with team members to develop a common (shared) definition for "intelligent risk taking" – to be used as a guideline for future activities.

38 Identify specific behaviors that encourage risk taking and those that discourage it. Make a commitment to adopt encouraging behaviors and avoid discouraging ones ... and ask others to do the same.

39 Turn failures into developmental experiences by asking:

What's positive about this?

What have we learned that will help us do better next time?

Bottom line: Make it okay to occasionally fail.

40 Recognize and celebrate intelligent risk taking – no matter the outcome. Make it something to brag about. Consider establishing an "Intelligent Risk Taker of the Month Award."

Resolve Disputes Fairly

*The hallmark of a well-managed organization
is not the absence of problems, but whether or not
problems are effectively resolved.*

~ Steve Ventura

41 Remember that "stuff" happens! Disputes are a natural outcome of individuals working together. So expect problems … and accept the challenge of resolving them as an opportunity to eliminate obstacles to organizational effectiveness.

42 Make sure your "open door" is really *open.* Encourage members of your work group to bring their complaints to you – and don't become defensive when they do.

43 Thoroughly investigate all team-member complaints and make a sincere effort to resolve them as quickly as possible. Handle them as your top priority on any given day … that's exactly what they are to the people who have them.

44 Focus on *what's* right rather than *who's* right. Don't let unrelated issues – or your feelings about certain people (positive or negative) – bias your decisions.

FREE ... How to Resolve Conflicts in a "C.A.L.M." Fashion

Go to *www.walkthetalk.com*
(Click on "Free Resources")

Positively Manage
Crisis Situations

A diamond is a chunk of coal that made good under pressure.
~ Anonymous

45 Approach crises as a team. Allow everyone to "own a piece" of the problem. Don't be an "overprotective parent" by trying to shield people. Capitalize on individual strengths and give everyone the opportunity to contribute to the solution.

46 Critically assess your behavior, and request feedback from others on how you handle crisis situations. Take responsibility for setting the tone … and the example. Realize that others will assume it's okay to respond to a crisis the same way you do.

47 *Over*-communicate to keep others informed and grind down the rumor mill. Consider implementing **5/3 Status Briefings** – five minute updates at the beginning, middle, and end of each day.

48 Conclude each crisis with a "Post-Mortem Celebration." Review what happened, identify key learning that can be applied in the future, and celebrate the accomplishment of getting through it together.

Provide Recognition

*There are two things that people want more than
sex and money – recognition and praise.*
~ Mary Kay Ash

49 **Be a Star Catcher.** Regularly "catch people doing things
right" and recognize them for it. And, make recognition self-
perpetuating by recognizing those who recognize others.
Remember ...

> **What gets recognized gets reinforced,
> and what gets reinforced gets repeated.**

50 Develop a list of at least 20 ways to recognize others for their
performance and contributions. Some ideas to get you started:
a Thank You e-card or Praise-A-Gram, small gifts, special
assignments, etc.

51 **Customize the recognition you provide.** Ask each member of
your team how you can best demonstrate your appreciation for
them. Then provide it!

52 Let everyone "hold the trophy." Be sure each contributing
member shares in the recognition for achievements.

Recognition Checklist

Make sure the recognition you provide is ...

 TIMELY
Don't wait. Give recognition as soon as possible after the good performance takes place. Praise tends to lose its effectiveness with the passing of time.

 SPECIFIC
Tell the person exactly what she/he did that was good. A mere "nice job" really doesn't say all that much. Being specific lets the person know what behaviors to repeat in the future.

 SINCERE
Insincere praise is usually worse than none at all. Be honest and open. Tell the person what their performance means to you personally.

 INDIVIDUAL
Focus on individuals rather than groups. Fact is, not all team members contribute equally.

 PERSONAL
Adjust the style and method of your recognition to the receiver. Some people like public praise ... some prefer private discussions. Give "different strokes to different folks." Not sure what they prefer? Ask!

 PROPORTIONAL
Match the amount and intensity of recognition to the achievement. Going overboard for small stuff will make people question your motives.

Coach Others

Coaching isn't an addition to a leader's job,
it's an integral part of it.
~ George S. Odiorne

53 **Pay attention to "middle stars."** Avoid the trap of focusing only on the "super stars" (those with exceptional performance) and the "fallen stars" (those with significant performance problems). Most team members shine somewhere in the middle.

54 Schedule a short meeting with the members of your team once every two to three weeks. Discuss their work-in-progress, provide feedback on how they're doing, and ask how you and others can contribute to their success.

55 **Go back to school!** Read web-articles or books, watch videos, listen to audio tapes, or attend a workshop that deals specifically with coaching techniques. Then apply what you learn.

56 Build an "Everyone's a Coach" environment. Begin by identifying the characteristics and behaviors exhibited by good coaches. Then ask everyone for their commitment to practice those behaviors with each other. Consider providing coaching-skills training to help each team member assume their new coaching role.

Conduct one-on-one meetings regularly.

Offer feedback and assistance.

Avoid overlooking the "middle stars."

Create an "Everyone's a Coach" environment.

Help others succeed.

Minimize Obstacles

All too frequently, employees do good work in spite of the organization and its leadership, rather than because of them.
~ Al Lucia

57 Ask each member of your work group to identify the three most significant obstacles to their performance. Create a master list and develop strategies to eliminate them. And, by all means, reward people for identifying obstacles. They've made a significant contribution by pinpointing ways you can add value and positively affect organizational effectiveness.

58 If you don't control an obstacle your work group is facing, talk to the people who do. Point out the impact and cost of the problem and discuss possible solutions. Even if you can't eliminate an obstacle, you may be able to minimize its effect by showing people how to get around it easier and less painfully.

59 Ask others what you may or may not be doing that creates obstacles for them. If they tell you, *thank* them for their honesty, don't get defensive, and take action to eliminate the obstacles you're creating.

60 **Benchmark the Best.** Study industries, organizations, and individuals who beat the competition by overcoming challenges and obstacles. Also, review case studies of those who did not … and lost.

Provide Feedback

Feedback is the breakfast of champions.
~ Ken Blanchard and Spencer Johnson
The One Minute Manager

61 Be certain that each team member fully understands your performance expectations. Feedback is most effective when people know the standards against which their performance is being measured.

62 Develop the habit of giving each member of your team some type of feedback every week. If you're apt to forget, put a tickler in your calendar or scheduling software.

63 Make sure your feedback passes the **TIPS Test**:

Timely
Given as soon as possible to the performance;
Individualized
Tailored to the feedback receiver;
Productive
Focuses on the performance, not the performer;
Specific
Pinpoints observable actions and behaviors.

64 **Solicit feedback on your feedback.** Ask others to critique your nonverbal (looks, behaviors, etc.) as well as verbal feedback. Keep in mind that body language often communicates stronger messages than do words.

Apply Rules Fairly
and Consistently

*Leaders who choose which rules to follow and
which ones to let slide set a dangerous example
for their people to follow. And they WILL follow!*
~ Steve Ventura

65 Make certain that all team members understand the importance of, reasons for, and specific details of work rules and organizational policies.

66 As a group, define the terms "fairness" and "consistency" as they relate to policy and rule application. Use those definitions as guidelines for yourself and others.

67 Don't ignore "bad" rules and policies. Instead, try to get them changed. Be sure you're fully prepared when proposing a change: Explain why the rule is problematic, describe how it negatively impacts business, and offer at least two alternatives for consideration.

68 Create a list of *Other Rules of the Road* (e.g., demonstrating respect for others, practicing open and honest communication, etc.) – and treat these equally as important as all other rules.

Address Deficiencies

*No one enjoys addressing others' deficiencies. But failure
to do so sends the message that people are on track when
they really aren't. And that may be the greatest disservice
a leader can do to someone else.*

~ Eric Harvey

69 Pay attention when someone has a performance problem.
Unaddressed deficiencies can have a negative effect on every
member of your team. By dealing with performance issues as
early as possible, you can prevent them from growing more
serious ... and more distasteful for both you and the individual
to face.

70 Investigate each deficiency to uncover its root cause. If the
problem stems from a lack of skills, arrange for skill-building
activities (formal training, on-the-job training, etc.). If there
is an obstacle to performance, attempt to eliminate it. If you
believe the person *can* perform properly but just isn't doing
so, review the standard and hold him or her accountable for
meeting it.

71 **Follow-up for follow-through!** Follow the initial performance
discussion with one or two short meetings to assess the
person's progress and encourage them to follow through with
the correction.

72 **Treat people as adults.** Never assume total responsibility for
correcting someone else's deficiencies. If you alone take the
responsibility, they become *non*-responsible.

Use Discipline Appropriately

Little value comes out of the belief that people will respond progressively better by treating them progressively worse.
~ Eric Harvey

73 **Try a positive approach to discipline.** (Yes, we did use "positive" and "discipline" in the same sentence!) Focus on correction and individual responsibility rather than blame and punishment. Avoid perspectives such as *write you up* and *punishment that fits the crime.*

74 When holding disciplinary discussions, concentrate on the particular problem and its impact on the business. Deal with specific facts and behaviors – not personality or attitude traits. This will help decrease defensiveness and produce value-added outcomes.

75 Never document a disciplinary problem without talking to the person about the issue. A good rule of thumb:

> **If it's important enough to document, it's definitely important enough to talk about.**

76 Apply discipline effectively by ensuring that: a) Your process and decisions are fair and consistent, and b) Your overall objective is to build commitment rather than to force people into compliance.

Perform with Integrity

If leaders are careless about basic things – telling the
truth, respecting moral codes, proper professional conduct –
who can believe them on other issues?
~ James L. Hayes

77 Everyone must play by the same rules. *Rank has its privileges* may apply in some circumstances, but never when it comes to justifying lapses in integrity.

78 Nobody's perfect. Everyone makes mistakes and errors in judgment – including YOU! When you do, admit to them and apologize for any negative impacts they may have caused. How you recover from mistakes is a true indication of your integrity.

79 **Be a person of your word.** Write down all promises and agreements you make … and honor them. Remember: One broken promise overshadows five promises kept.

80 **Let your conscience be your guide.** Do the right thing no matter how inconvenient, unpopular, or painful it may seem. *That's* integrity!

FREE … Top 10 Characteristics of Ethical Leaders and Values-Driven Organizations

Go to *www.walkthetalk.com*
(Click on "Free Resources")

The Ethical Action Test

Check each decision and planned action for "rightness" *before* implementing it. Use the questions below (or similar ones supplied by your organization) as your litmus test. Answering "no" to one or more of the following would suggest the need to either develop an alternate strategy or to seek counsel and advice from appropriate sources:

A. Is it legal?

B. Does it comply with our rules and guidelines?

C. Is it in sync with our organizational values?

D. Will I be comfortable and guilt-free if I do it?

E. Does it match our stated commitments and guarantees?

F. Would I do it to my family or friends?

G. Would I be perfectly okay with someone doing it to me?

H. Would the most ethical person I know do it?

Support
Organizational Values

*It's critical that leaders ensure their departments and teams
are about what the organization says IT is about.*
~ Al Lucia

81 Provide everyone with a copy of your mission, vision, and
values (or your organization's equivalents). Adopt the mindset
that these guidelines are as important as your work rules ...
and treat them accordingly.

82 Enlist your staff in a "Values Patrol." Solicit their commitment
to tell each other (including you) whenever they observe
behaviors or decisions they believe are out of sync with
organizational values. Have fun with this. Appoint a "Values
Officer" for important meetings. Supply him or her with a
toy police badge and a whistle to blow when values
violations are observed.

83 Develop a list of ways to recognize/reward team members
for behavior that's in sync with organizational values.
Continue working on your list until you have 15 ways –
then start doing them.

84 When planning projects and activities, write down what you
intend to accomplish, then add the phrase: *" ... in a way that
supports and furthers our organizational values."* Evaluate
your final plans – and eventual results – against this add-on
criterion.

Accept and Meet Responsibilities

Success on any major scale requires you to accept responsibility.
In the final analysis, the one quality that all successful
people have is the ability to take on responsibility.
~ Michael Korda

85 Ensure everyone's responsibilities, *including yours*, are clearly defined and commonly understood. Whether it's a specific project or general job duty, don't assume that people know who's responsible for what ... discuss it!

86 **Be selfish!** Never share the blame for your mistakes.

87 Volunteer to take on additional responsibilities and duties – especially when no one else wants them. This may temporarily result in more work for you and your group, but it may also provide opportunities to develop individuals and have a greater influence on important outcomes for your organization. And your gesture just might compel others to do the same.

88 **Check the mirror first!** Make sure you're meeting all of *your* responsibilities before holding others accountable for meeting theirs.

Handle Authority Appropriately

Being powerful is like being a lady.
If you have to tell people you are, you aren't.
~ Margaret Thatcher

89 Adopt the mindset that your employees don't work for you – you work for them. Refer to your team members as: *the people I work for.*

90 Avoid "my way or the highway" thinking and behaviors. They're counterproductive and limit the possibilities of discovering new and better ways to do things. And, your competitors just may be looking to pick up hitchhikers!

91 Complete the sentence: *"I do my most effective work for leaders who ... "* List as many answers as possible and use this list as your guide to leading others.

92 Remember that with authority comes the responsibility to use it wisely, sparingly, and for the benefit of your entire team. The organization can bestow a leadership title, but it's up to you to really *earn* it.

Empower Others

The best [leader] is the one who has sense enough to pick good
[people] to do what [he/she] wants done, and self-restraint enough
to keep from meddling with them while they do it.
~ Theodore Roosevelt

93 **Share authority.** Let each team member be the "owner" of something meaningful – like a process, a database, a piece of equipment, a room in your facility, etc. Having real (and recognized) authority changes the scope and perception of a responsibility that is already part of the job description.

94 Create opportunities for nonmanagerial employees to shine. Invite them to participate in – or even lead – task forces and project teams. The often untapped potential of this group is one of your organization's greatest hidden assets.

95 Never turn your back on people after giving them authority. Instead, *increase* communication, feedback, and interaction. Make sure they understand the parameters and expectations of that authority. And, help them be successful by providing the resources and support they need.

96 Speak EMPOWERESE. Add statements, like these, to your vocabulary:

Would you like to take the lead on this one?
How can I best support you?
It's your call!
I trust your judgment.

Support Teamwork

Alone we can do so little; together we can do so much.
~ Helen Keller

97 Accept the reality that team approaches may take longer – but they usually add more value and produce better results in the long run.

98 **Make teamwork a stated performance expectation.** Involve others in compiling a list of factors and characteristics critical to effective teamwork. Then, hold people accountable for cooperative behaviors and for contributing to one another's success.

99 Provide training and coaching to help individuals work effectively in teams. Don't assume people can or will work as a team merely because you have labeled them as one.

100 Recruit and select people who have walk-in teamwork behaviors. It's difficult enough to change attitudes and behaviors of existing employees, much less compounding the problem by adding new human obstacles.

FREE Survey ... What Kind of Team Player Am I?

Go to *www.walkthetalk.com*
(Click on "Free Resources")

Our job descriptions
identify the specific functions
we perform.

Our **VALUES** describe
how we should perform
those functions.

Enhance the Work Environment

The quality of employees will be directly proportional to the quality of life you maintain for them.
~ Charles E. Bryan

101 Hold everyone accountable for doing their jobs so that no one has to pick up the slack for others.

102 Ask each team member to submit three ideas for enhancing the quality of work life in your area. Create a master list of ideas and start implementing the doable ones as quickly as possible.

103 Make "Quality of Work Life" a periodic agenda item for staff/ team meetings. Solicit feedback on how the group is doing and where you can make improvements.

104 Recruit someone to be your group's "Ambassador of Fun." Make appropriate resources available for them to help bring enjoyment to the workplace. Consider rotating the responsibility every few months.

See
"The Big Picture"

You've got to think about "big things" while you're doing small
things, so that all the small things go in the right direction.
~ Alvin Toffler

105 Keep this in mind: Everything that you and your team
members do either adds value and supports your organization's mission ... or it doesn't. Too many of the latter, and
people may begin to question the value of your contributions.

106 Identify and consider all sides of an issue before making a
decision or planning work activities. Ask yourself:

> *How will this action affect other departments,*
> *individual team members, our customers,*
> *and the organization as a whole?*

107 Involve others in developing a mission statement for your
business unit. Make sure it's a subset of the organization's
overall mission ... and that it describes your unit's specific
contribution and supporting activities.

108 **Take a field trip.** Let your team see "the big picture" for
themselves by visiting other departments within your
company and end users of your products and services.

Be Enthusiastic

If you're working in a company that is not ENTHUSIASTIC,
energetic, creative, clever, curious, and just plain fun,
you've got troubles, serious troubles.
~ Tom Peters

109 **Get excited about positive things.** If you're normally calm and reserved, pick something you're "fired-up" about and act yourself into excitement. Initiate enthusiasm and the feeling will follow!

110 Think of the most enthusiastic person you know. Ask him or her to share their secrets to maintaining an enthusiastic outlook. Then, practice those secrets ... and pass them along to others.

111 Enlist the help of others to build a "pump-you-up" library. Include motivational books, audio and video tapes, a list of websites offering inspirational material, etc. Encourage everyone on the team to take advantage of these resources.

112 **Spread the Sparkle.** Get enthused about others who are enthusiastic – it's contagious and can snowball quickly. Recognize and reward those who help contribute to a culture of contagious enthusiasm.

Display Resilience

It's not whether you get knocked down, it's whether you get up.
~ Vince Lombardi

When facing disappointment or frustration ...

113 Take a deep breath, slowly count to fifteen, and think about how you want to affect others. Your responsibility is to lead people *out* of disappointment, not into it.

114 **Take a hike!** Go on a ten-minute walk to calm down, reflect, and develop a bounce-back strategy.

115 Maintain the proper perspective: It's not the end of the world, so don't act like it is. Find one or two positives and keep thinking about them until you feel better. Then move on to other tasks.

When dealing with worries ...

116 **Try *celebrating* your worries!** Create a "Worry Jar" ... each time you have a worry, write it down and place it in the jar. Take time every week to open the jar and worry about all your worries. When you get tired of worrying about something, remove it from the jar. Over time, you'll have fewer and fewer worries.

Show Concern
for Others

*When people work in a place that cares about them,
they contribute a lot more than duty.*
~ Dennis Hayes

117   **Remember special occasions.** Send cards, e-cards, or notes
with personalized messages to your team members on special
days such as birthdays and anniversaries with the organization.

118   Regularly spend one-on-one time with each member of
your team. Open these informal get-togethers with a general
question like: *How are things going with you?* Then, really
listen to what they have to say. Listening is an important
way to demonstrate that you care.

119   Whenever possible, help people balance work needs and
personal needs. A little consideration and flexibility on your
part can go a long way in showing you care for others beyond
just what they can produce on the job.

120   **Walk a mile in their shoes!** Periodically "tag along" with
members of your team and observe, firsthand, the issues and
problems they face. You'll be better able to see and understand
things from their perspective ... and develop the empathy
important to caring for others.

Solicit and Apply
Feedback from Others

Truly great leaders spend as much time collecting and
acting on feedback as they do providing it.
~ Al Lucia

121 Don't wait for your annual appraisal to collect feedback on your performance. Ask your boss to meet with you at least once each quarter to discuss how you're doing.

122 Ask others in your sphere of influence to become partners in your efforts for continuous improvement. Regularly solicit feedback on how you are perceived. Then seek out a "Coaching Buddy" or mentor to help you sort through this information and develop action plans to increase your effectiveness.

123 **Keep a Feedback Log.** Dedicate a page in your calendar, scheduling software, PDA, etc., to record feedback you receive from others ... and the specific things you will do to ACT upon that feedback. Review the log at the beginning of each week.

124 Circulate your first-draft work among appropriate individuals with a request for upgrade suggestions. Try to incorporate as many ideas as possible into your final product. Don't forget to show your appreciation to your reviewers for their time and contributions. You'll end up with a better product ... and you'll enhance your relationships with others.

Manage Time

*Time is the scarcest resource, and unless it is
managed, nothing else can be managed.*
~ Peter F. Drucker

125   **Target the "Time Wasters."** Work with team members to
identify all inefficient uses of time existing within your area.
Select the three most significant items and develop a joint
strategy for eliminating or minimizing them.

126   Delegate important tasks you don't have time to do. Just
make sure you're not creating unnecessary work for, or over-
burdening, others. Keep in mind that everyone is responsible
for helping everyone else manage time effectively.

127   Tackle your "in-basket" and non-critical e-mail every *other*
day instead of every day. Focus on completing the really
important items rather than trying to stay caught up each day.
Ask others to "flag" high-priority items that require immedi-
ate attention.

128   **Go on vacation** ... an *in-office vacation*. Isolate yourself in
order to work on critical projects and ask others to handle
issues as if you really were gone. Clear it with your boss ...
and ask for his or her cooperation in honoring your "time off."

Manage Meetings

The form of the meeting is simply a reflection of the culture.
~ Terrence Deal & Allan Kennedy
Corporate Cultures

129 **Does it make \$en\$e to have a meeting?** Don't have a meeting if there's a more cost-effective way to achieve your objective. Ask others to help you develop a list of ways to accomplish tasks with minimal need for group meetings. Just for fun: Calculate the total cost of your last meeting (salaries plus other expenses) and see if you got your money's worth.

130 Supply all participants with a written agenda two to three days prior to each meeting. Make sure the agenda includes meeting objective(s), issues to be discussed, start/end times and location, who will be attending, how participants should prepare, and what they should bring.

131 **Manage the meeting.** Establish ground rules up front – including a list of "do" and "don't" meeting behaviors. Then keep the group on track, follow the ground rules, and adhere to the time frame. If you manage the process, the results will often take care of themselves.

132 End all meetings with a short review of results. Discuss what was accomplished – and what, if anything, needs to be done after the meeting (by *when* … and by *whom*).

Communicate Effectively

The art of communication is the language of leadership.
~ James Humes

133 **Think before you speak ... and plan before you write.**
Understand your message *before* expecting understanding from
others. Target your communication to the intended audience
by using terminology they are likely to understand. Consider
"pre-testing" important communications on individuals whom
you trust to give you candid feedback.

134 **Be concise and specific.** Avoid ambiguous words and
phrases that may mean different things to different people
(e.g. *usually, sometimes, a lot, rarely,* etc.).

135 Use "Right Brain Messages." Try communicating *creatively*
with stories, examples, pictures, props, etc., to help convey
your message and increase retention.

136 Never assume others understand what you say or write.
Check to be sure! Ask people to describe their understanding
of your message. This will allow you to clarify and correct
any mis-understandings.

The Important
Words of Leadership

10 important words:
What can I do to help you be more successful?

9 important words:
I need you to do this, and here's why ...

8 important words:
That's my mistake and I will fix it.

7 important words:
My door is always open to you.

6 important words:
Let's focus on solving the problem.

5 important words:
You did a great job!

4 important words:
What do YOU think?

3 important words:
Follow my lead.

2 important words:
Thank You.

Perhaps the **MOST** important word:
YOU.

Keep Others Informed

If you don't give people information, they'll make up something to fill the void.
~ Carla O'Dell

137 Establish a "No Surprise Rule" for yourself and others. Make withholding bad news one of the absolute worst violations of all.

138 Don't be an information-hoarding "Power Broker." Ask your team members to identify the kind and amount of information that would help them be more successful ... and – as long as it's not confidential in nature – make sure they get it.

139 Regularly update your boss and colleagues on your team's activities and progress. That way, if anyone has a problem with where you're headed, you'll find out *before* going too far down the wrong path.

140 Designate an area to be your "Information Central." Provide bulletin boards – or a site on your organization's intranet for displaying activities in progress, results, project status, production data, new products, and other general information.

FREE ... The four critical dimensions of communication that are so often overlooked

Go to *www.walkthetalk.com*
(Click on "Free Resources")

Listen to Others

Nature has given us two ears, two eyes, and but one tongue –
to the end that we should hear and see more than we speak.
~ Socrates

141 Give each speaker your conscious attention. Maintain eye contact and listen for feelings as well as words. This will help you absorb the full extent of their communication and make them feel important at the same time.

142 **Paraphrase** – repeat back in your own words what the person says. Paraphrasing typically begins with:

> ### *What I hear you saying is ...*
> ### and ends with:
> ### *Is that correct?*

143 Make listening a highly valued attribute for your work group. Provide listening skills training for everyone, and focus on setting the listening example. In this case, you *EARn* the right to be heard by listening to others.

144 **NEVER ...**
   ... interrupt someone when they're speaking.
   ... plan what you'll say while they're talking.
   ... assume you are listening just because you can hear.

144 Plus

Your personal list of **Additional Ways to WALK THE TALK:**

_____

_____

_____

_____

_____

_____

_____

_____

_____

_____

_____

_____

_____

_____

_____

_____

Our efforts to do a better
job of living our values will
undoubtedly come with flaws.

But, if we meet those flaws
and occasional failures with
both persistence and patience,
we can unlock the fortunes that
exist within our organizations.

The Publisher

Since 1977, **The WALK THE TALK® Company (WalkTheTalk.com)** has helped organizations, worldwide, achieve success through values-based practices. Our goal is both simple and straightforward: *To provide you and your organization with high-impact resources for your personal and professional success.*

Visit us at **WalkTheTalk.com** to learn more about our:

- ▶ Leadership & Employee Development Centre
- ▶ Inspired Living Café
- ▶ Motivational Gift Books
- ▶ FREE Online Newsletters
- ▶ Inspirational Movies
- ▶ 360° Feedback Processes
- ▶ Personal Development Kits
- ▶ *And much more!*

Contact The **WALK THE TALK Team** at **1.888.822.9255**
Or visit us at *www.walkthetalk.com*

The Authors

Eric Harvey is president and founder of WalkTheTalk.com and author of 30 highly acclaimed books – including the best-selling *WALK THE TALK ... And Get The Results You Want, Ethics4Everyone,* and *The Leadership Secrets of Santa Claus.*

Al Lucia, CSP – "America's Lifeline to The People Side of Business" – is a respected speaker, consultant, author, and coach who specializes in building employee engagement and commitment.

WALK THE TALK® Resources

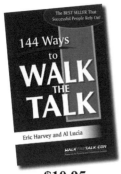

Better yet, consider ...

The WALK THE TALK®
Development Kit
for you and your colleagues

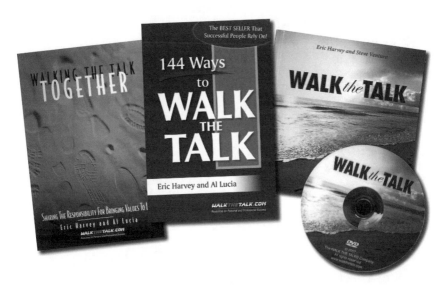

This kit contains the following resources:

- ▶ **144 Ways to Walk The Talk**
- ▶ **Walking The Talk Together**
- ▶ **WALK *the* TALK Gift Book**
  - *and*
- ▶ **<u>New</u> WALK *the* TALK Inspirational Movie**

All for only $34.95!

To order, visit **WalkTheTalk.com**

Visit **WalkTheTalk.com**
and Sign Up for our
FREE Online Newsletters

My Daily Inspiration
Powerful Inspiring Messages to "kick start" your day.

Monday Morning Must-Read
Straight-talk tips for employee success.

The Power of Inspiration
A weekly newsletter designed to uplift, inspire,
and motivate you … and the important people in your life.

The Leadership Solution
Weekly tips to help you and your colleagues become
more effective and respected leaders.

Inspired Living
Stretch Your Mind, Nourish Your Soul, Gladden
Your Heart.

Be sure to visit **WalkTheTalk.com**
to view our complete library of

And while you are visiting
WalkTheTalk.com
take a moment to learn more about our

Personal Development Kits
Each designed to build skills and motivate individuals to achieve higher levels of personal effectiveness.

Group Training Programs
Comprehensive training packages based on best-selling WALK THE TALK books – ranging from *Ethics4Everyone* and *Positive Discipline,* to *Five Star Teamwork* and *Ouch! That Stereotype Hurts.*

360° <u>Online</u> Feedback Process
A fast and affordable 360° feedback process. Each participating leader will receive a comprehensive personal profile outlining his or her performance strengths and developmental opportunities – plus resources to help turn their information into ACTION!

WalkTheTalk.com
1.888.822.9255

ORDER FORM

*Have questions? Need assistance? Call **1.888.822.9255***

☑ **Please send me extra copies of:** *144 Ways to Walk The Talk*

1-99 copies $10.95 each   100-499 copies $9.95 each   500+ copies please call

144 Ways to Walk The Talk	____ copies X	_____	=$_____
Walking The Talk Together	____ copies X	$ 10.95	=$_____
WALK *the* TALK Gift Book & Movie	____ sets X	$ 15.95	=$_____
WALK THE TALK Development Kit	____ sets X	$ 34.95	=$_____

Product Total	$_____
*Shipping & Handling	$_____
Subtotal	$_____

Sales Tax:

(Tax Collected on TX Customers Only)

Texas Sales Tax - 8.25%	$_____
Total (U.S. Dollars Only)	$_____

---

*Shipping and Handling Charges

For actual shipping rates, please visit *WalkTheTalk.com*

Name_____ Title_____

Organization_____

Shipping Address_____

City_____ State_____ Zip _____
      (No PO Boxes)

Phone_____ Fax_____

E-Mail:_____

Charge Your Order: ☐ MasterCard   ☐ Visa   ☐ American Express

Credit Card Number_____ Exp. Date_____

☐ Check Enclosed (Payable to The WALK THE TALK Company)

☐ Please Invoice (**Orders over $250 ONLY**)   ☐ P.O. Number (required)_____

WALKTHETALK.COM
Resources for Personal and Professional Success

PHONE	ONLINE	MAIL
PHONE 1.888.822.9255 or 972.899.8300 M-F, 8:30-5:00 Cen.	**ONLINE** www.walkthetalk.com **FAX** 972.899.9291	**MAIL** WALK THE TALK Co. 1100 Parker Square, Suite 250 Flower Mound, TX 75028

Prices effective March 2009 are subject to change.